TA...
TIKKA DISHES

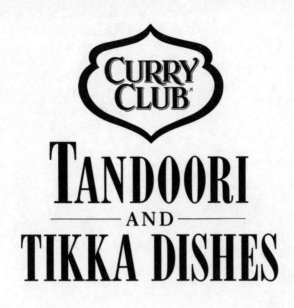

CURRY CLUB

TANDOORI

— AND —

TIKKA DISHES

PAT CHAPMAN

PIATKUS

© 1993 Pat Chapman

First published in 1993 by
Judy Piatkus (Publishers) Limited
5 Windmill Street, London W1P 1HF

The moral right of the author has been asserted

A catalogue record for this book
is available from the British Library

ISBN 0-7499-1283-9

Designed by Sue Ryall
Photography by James Murphy

Typeset by Computerset, Harmondsworth, Heathrow
Printed and bound in Great Britain by
Mackays of Chatham PLC

Contents

Foreword

THE CURRY CLUB

Since it was founded in January 1982, The Curry Club has built up a membership of several thousands. Members receive a bright and colourful magazine four times a year, which has regular features on curry and the curry lands. It includes news items, recipes, reports on restaurants, picture features and contributions from members and professionals alike. We have produced a wide selection of publications, including the books on page ii.

Obtaining the ingredients required for Indian cooking can be difficult, but The Curry Club makes it easy, with a comprehensive range of Curry Club products, including spice mixes, chutneys, pickles, papadoms, sauces and curry pastes. These are available from major food stores and specialist delicatessens up and down the country. If they are not stocked near you, there is the Club's well-established and efficient mail-order service. Hundreds of items are stocked, including spices, pastes, gift items, publications and specialist kitchen and tableware.

The Club also holds residential weekend cookery courses and gourmet nights at selected restaurants. Top of the list is our regular gourmet trip to India and other spicy countries. We take a small group of curry enthusiasts to the chosen country and tour the incredible sights, in between sampling the delicious foods of each region.

If you would like more information about **The Curry Club**, write (enclosing a SAE) to: **The Curry Club, PO Box 7, Haslemere, Surrey GU27 1EP.**

Introduction

Britain's first recorded invasion took place 2,000 years ago when Julius Caesar spearheaded a highly sophisticated occupation that made England into the most distant part of the Roman empire, and which lasted 400 years. The subsequent invasions from the Saxons, Danes and Vikings were rather less civilised but they too left their indelible marks on the nation. The Norman conquest of 1066 was the final invasion to succeed and despite attempts from the Spanish, French and Germans we have remained a stubborn, insular, wealthy, arrogant, defiant, self-critical, conservative nation, highly resistant to change, and very suspicious of it.

These qualities resulted in the establishment of the world's most successful and comprehensive empire and a reputation of invincibility. Our culinary reputation was never placed into higher echelons; indeed most nations thought British food to be bland and totally unworthy of tasting. Both reputations were short of the mark. We were not invincible and our indigenous food can be exquisite when kept out of the hands of canteen caterers and mass producers. However, until just a few decades ago garlic was an ingredient which was hard to obtain and which appeared in no British food, and the few spices we used were the likes of cloves, pepper, mustard and caraway.

It may be because of this gap that the arrival and growth of ethnic restaurants, especially curry and tandoori houses has been so spectacularly rapid nationwide. In 1946, just after the war there were just six Indian restaurants in the whole of Great Britain. Only one,

Veeraswamy in Regent Street, had any mention of tandoori. On their menu dating from the early 1950s, 'Tunduri Chicken' cost 2/6d ($12^1/_2$ pence in today's money), which was considered expensive then. But they had no tandoor oven – and the trend which was to sweep the country had not yet begun. It would be the 1970s before it began in earnest. Yet by 1993 of the 7,500 curry houses in the UK over 95 per cent describe themselves as tandoori restaurants. There are now nearly as many such establishments in the British Isles as there are fish and chip shops or chemists. And there are far more here than in the whole of India.

Over the last 20 years, from a starting point of virtually zero to near saturation of the nation, an invasion has finally succeeded after 900 years . . . the tandoori invasion. It is total, peaceful, popular and probably irreversible. It too has left an indelible mark on the nation. Its effect on the indigenous population has been transmogrifying. We are a nation of tandoori addicts.

Food is arguably the most successful route to multiracial integration, and if Britain's empire achieved anything it has led to a remarkable conversion of the British palate. We still adore our roasts and our fry-ups, our fish and chips and our steak and kidney puds, but we have the added advantage of access to a wealth of extra choice available from our ethnic restaurants, our supermarkets and our delicatessens.

The tandoori invasion of Britain is one of the world's culinary outstanding success stories.

And it is a story which has not reached its conclusion yet. Statistics reveal that over 60 per cent of the population enjoy tandoori dishes regularly. But they also show that a stubborn 8 per cent have not tried tandoori, or curry, or Chinese, or indeed any ethnic food. They detest garlic though they are unlikely to have ever eaten it and nothing, they say, will convert them.

The interesting facts are that tandoori is immensely popular with an increasingly younger age group, and of the remaining 30 per cent (who have never, or rarely, tasted its delights) fortunately there are thousands converted daily. By my reckoning the invasion and my job will not be complete until 100 per cent enjoy the delights of tandoori food as a regular part of their diet. As a user of this book you will almost certainly be a convert, and I hope its contents will enable you to explore possibilities to greater depths. In particular, I hope you'll cook from this book for your friends and guests. There is no better introduction to the food of the Indian subcontinent than tandoori food. I pray you'll make some converts yourself.

WHAT ARE TANDOORI AND TIKKA?

Tandoori cooking is a unique method of cooking food (meat, poultry, seafood or vegetables) over a charcoal heat source, controlled inside a purpose-built 'oven' called the **tandoor**. The food is coated with a thick sauce comprising of yoghurt and spices and marinated overnight to allow the flavours to penetrate and the meat or chicken to become tenderised.

The marinated food, such as a whole chicken, leg of lamb or whole fish, is then threaded on to a long **skewer** and placed in the tandoor. Its design results in an efficient stream of very hot air flowing past the item and cooking it. The food can also be cut into small cubes (**tikkas**) prior to marinating. A further variation, the **sheek kebab**, requires the meat to be pounded or ground with spices. No marination takes place before the meat is moulded on to the skewer and cooked in the tandoor. A particular type of flat leavened bread **naan** or **nan** is also tandoori cooked and is the traditional accompaniment along with fresh chutneys, salad and lemon wedges.

Tandoori cooking achieves its exquisite tastes from a combination of the marinade and the flavour that the tandoori heated charcoal imparts into the subject. And I have to admit that without a tandoor you will not achieve exactly the same flavour. It comes somewhere near, and makes an excellent subject when cooked over barbecue coals, and my recipes allow for this style of cooking. Domestic sized tandoors are available and serious tandoori addicts use them with great success at home. If you feel that you would like to obtain one, I give information on how to do so on page xiv. Most people, however, wish to achieve good results using their normal cooking appliance, so all my recipes are designed to cook in this way using the grill or main oven.

A LITTLE HISTORY

From the moment pre-historic man learned to harness fire, he cooked the wild animals and fowl he hunted by suspending their carcasses over a slow fire. The transition from hunting to herding gradually resulted in greater sophistication in the cookery department.

By 1500 BC, the Egyptians had invented the oven. Called the 'tonir', it was hemispherical and made of clay, with a side tunnel large enough to allow bread discs to be slid into the main oven. Before long much of the ancient world had learned to make leavened (rising) bread in the form of flat loaves. There is no evidence, however, to indicate that leavened bread and ovens had reached India until many centuries later.

It is entirely conceivable that it was the Moghuls who perfected Indian tandoori cooking, as they did with their entire range of dishes such as Korma, Rhogan Gosht, Biriani and Kofta dishes. But it is unlikely that they invented it. It is much more probable that early Turk, Persian and Arab Moslem invaders of the eighth and ninth century brought kebabs and charcoal cooking with them as they came through the passes of Persia and Afghanistan to become established in the rugged and mountainous areas of what is now called The North West Frontier in Pakistan and to evolve over the next few hundred years into the delicious cooking style we know today. The marinades became highly spiced and colourful, and yoghurt was incorporated to improve the marination process, particularly to assist with the tenderising of the meat or poultry, usually very tough. But the biggest transformation took place to the tonir. From a side entry hemisphere, it became a sphere with a narrow-necked opening at the top. It became the tandoor.

Tandoori cooking had clearly become established by 1483 when Babur conquered India and established the dynasty of Moghul emperors. There is ample written evidence to prove that the cooking style had been established in the emperors' main fortress courts of Agra, Delhi, Kashmir and Lahore. Upon the demise of the emperors in the eighteenth century tandoori technology and know-how, simple though it was, almost disappeared.

Fortunately for the world, tandoori cooking survived where it had begun in the North West Frontier area. Following the partition of India and Pakistan in 1947, one successful Indian Hindu restaurateur, fearing Moslem violence, closed his tandoori restaurant in Lahore and moved to Delhi. Strangely enough tandoori cooking was virtually unknown in post-partition India. The tradition for eating out in restaurants was confined to tourists and adventurous Indians in those days (it is still not a widely accepted activity there), but the Moti Mahal immediately became one of Delhi's talking points, with its flavourful colourful tandoori food.

TANDOORI TECHNOLOGY

The magic which is tandoori comes from the ingredients in the marinade, and of course from the tandoor, the oven which is purpose built to cook tandoori to perfection. As we have seen the tandoor evolved many centuries ago. I have heard it described as 'simplicity itself'. In fact this is an overstatement.

The tandoori is a large pottery tub, which is more or less spherical with an opening in the top. More accurately it is an oblate-spheroid (or egg shaped). The diagram below shows the principle. The professional version as used in the tandoori restaurant averages 3 feet (nearly 1 metre) high and 2 feet 6 inches (75 cm) in diameter. The opening at the top is about one foot (30 cm) in diameter. It is hand 'thrown' in one continuous operation (no mean feat in itself) from a special blend of clay, some of which is only found in the East. Bangladeshi jute is incorporated into the walls (which are about 2 inches/5 cm thick) to reinforce them. In village Pakistan, the tandoors are buried in the ground, the earth being packed tightly around them, to give heat insulation and stability. In the restaurant this is not practical (or comfortable to operate) so the clay oven is securely located in a square enclosure of fire brick insulation blocks. The open cavities are packed with high density glass-fibre wool insulation. A concrete top and ceramic tiles on the top and outside

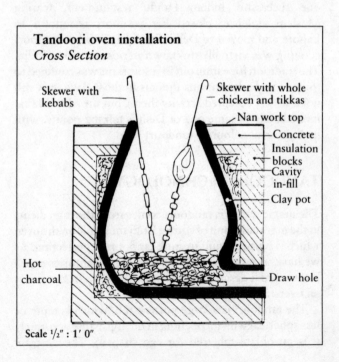

Tandoori oven installation
Cross Section

Skewer with kebabs

Skewer with whole chicken and tikkas

Nan work top

Concrete

Insulation blocks

Cavity in-fill

Clay pot

Hot charcoal

Draw hole

Scale ½″ : 1′ 0″

faces creates a hygienic kitchen appliance, cold on the outside yet very hot inside.

The oven is supplied unfired. (After three or four uses it has becomed fired). A small draw hole at the base can be opened or closed to create an air flow. Charcoal is the traditional fuel, and this is loaded in to about 6 inches (15 cm) in depth. It must then be allowed $2^1/_2$ to 3 hours to reach its operating temperature, by which time it is literally white hot (700°F/370°C). This extraordinarily high temperature is achieved by minimising heat loss (which maximises the efficiency of the fuel combustion), by the totally effective insulation described above.

It is a property of the special clay blend that it can withstand this high temperature without cracking, and the coals can be allowed to extinguish and the oven to go cold between usages with no shrinkage.

The only other implements a tandoori chef requires are a metal lid to cover the oven's opening to retain heat while the oven is 'at rest', and several long skewers. These are about 3 feet (90 cm) in length and have a square profile of about $^1/_2$ inch (1.25 cm) square. (Round skewers cause the food to rotate on them when turned).

The tandoori boom swept across Britain in the 1970s, when every curry house claimed to be a tandoori house whether it owned a tandoor or not. But those days have gone and every restaurant usually has not one but two tandoors, one charcoal fired running at high temperatures, and the other gas powered operating at lower temperatures.

Despite wild claims from exuberant restaurant proprietors that they import their tandoors from India, most of them are made in a purpose-built factory in London.

The main supplier of tandoor ovens to restaurants in Britain and Europe is Shah Gulian. Originally from Armenia, he was brought up in Cyprus and qualified in architecture, fine arts and pottery at Cheltenham College in 1969. He runs an architect's practice. He designed an Indian restaurant in Hendon in the early 1970s. The owner particularly wanted a tandoor. At the time they were available only from India. Gulian set about perfecting a design of his own. Today his team produce more than 800 each year.

DOMESTIC TANDOORS

A few years ago I asked Shah whether it would be possible to produce a small tandoor for domestic use. Within weeks he turned up with a delightful mini-version especially designed for home use. It is charcoal fired, easy to use and inexpensive. It is easy to move, can be set up anywhere and produces delicious authentic tandooris.

It comes complete on its own as a clay oven, or enclosed in fire bricks in a stainless steel wheeled box. It can be used indoors or out (but must not be allowed to get wet). Its size is about 1 foot 6 inches (38 cm), high and 1 foot 3 inches (31 cm) in diameter.

It is available from **Shah Gulian, The Tandoori Clay Oven Company Ltd, 1 Hassop Road, London, NW2 6RX. Telephone: 081 450 2847 or 018 204 3146.**

Serious tandoori cooks are well advised to acquire one of these units. At under £300 they will soon earn their keep.

AT THE RESTAURANT

If you haven't seen the tandoori chef at work at your favourite tandoori house, my advice is that you ask to have a look into the kitchens. Good restaurants have nothing to hide, and will welcome your interest in their work. Make sure you see the colourful marinades (the reds and oranges enhanced by food colouring) and see the long skewers being threaded and inserted into the tandoor. And don't miss the naan-bread making. The chef will slap it between the palms of the hands to obtain a flat disc. He then presses it directly on to the top wall of the oven. Remarkably it sticks there for the couple of minutes it takes to cook, elongating because of gravity into the familiar tear shape. Usually the chef uses a damp cloth to put the naan into place, but at one restaurant, **The Royal Naim Balti House** in Birmingham, where they specialise in gigantic naans the size of an elephant's ear, they use a damp pillow to press it into place. Some restaurants have glass fronted kitchens and you can view this work.

And the whereabouts of the best tandoori restaurant in the world? In my view it's the **Bukhara** at the **Maurya Sheraton Hotel in Delhi**. It seats about one hundred diners. It's always full with people queuing. Eight chefs are on view with at least six tandoor ovens in the glass-fronted kitchen. The food they turn out with great dexterity and speed before your very eyes is just exquisite.

ALTERNATIVE COOKING METHODS

Don't worry if you haven't got a tandoor because all the recipes in this book are written assuming the cook does not have either a tandoor or a barbecue set.

ABOUT FOOD COLOURING

Authentic tandooris and tikkas in India have always been cooked with natural colourings. Red is achieved using paprika or chilli. Deep red is from a root called *ratin jot*. Yellow comes from saffron and turmeric. There is no natural orange. I have used anatto seed powder for yellow orange, and beetroot powder for deep red (see page 6). These can be obtained by post (see page vi). All these natural colours are not heat stable, so they can change colour (becoming browner) when cooked, although the colours of the finished dishes are, in my view, perfectly attractive and natural.

The very bright reds and oranges that we are accustomed to at the tandoori house, are frankly pure boloney. They are, of course, tartrazine food dyes. Made from coal tar, they are said to have 'side effects' on a few children causing allergies and hyperactivity. However, those who wish to achieve these vibrant colours can use food colourings, in powdered form (available by post, page vi) if they wish. They do not affect the taste of the dish, but are very concentrated, so use just a tiny bit.

WHAT TO SERVE WITH TANDOORI AND TIKKA

Tandoori and tikkas are served as a starter or as a main course. Portions for a starter are smaller. Both are superb with a bed of salad. This can be much more exciting than just lettuce. There are plenty of ideas on page 16. Naan bread is almost obligatory and several versions are given between pages 60 and 63. Yoghurt-based chutney (raita) and bottled chutneys and pickles go very well. I personally adore raw onion rings and fresh onion chutney (cachumber) with tandoori dishes.

For those who want rice as well as or instead of naan bread, there are two variations on pages 58 and 59. In my other curry books listed (on page ii) you will find a greater selection or rice, bread, lentils and chutney accompaniments, most of them not hot.

DRINK

This is a personal choice. I like red wine with tandooris and curries although experts disagree about this. It should not be fine wine – a cheap and cheerful plonk will do the meal great justice in my view. Rosé, white wine, sparkling wine and real ale are also appropriate. Most lagers are too gassy, although Cobra Lager brewed in Bangalore is designed to go with curry. Non alcoholic drinks are always acceptable.

CHAPTER · 1

Ingredients
and Basic Recipes

INGREDIENTS

Most of the fresh and dried ingredients in this book are widely available from supermarkets and delicatessens. If you do have problems obtaining any of the specialist ingredients or equipment such as ghee, coconut milk, tamarind, sizzler dishes and of course all the spices listed below, they are available, along with much much more, by mail order, see page vi.

SPICES

It is the combination of spices which makes the cooking of the sub-continent of India so special. Tandoori cooking is no exception and the spices you will need to make these recipes are not too many; neither will they cost you too much. Yet they are crucial to all which follows, so they should be cared for as if they were gold. There are some rules on page 2.

Opposite page xvi: Tandoori Bhare Murgh (**pages 30-1**), Naan Bread (**page 60**), and Onion Salad – Cachumber (**page 57**)

Overleaf: a full-sized tandoor in operation, with cooked Sheek Kebabs (**page 21**), Tikkas (**page 18**), a whole Tandoori Chicken (**page 30**), and Tandoori Chicken Legs (**page 29**) being lifted out. Note the unused clay tandoor to the left

Opposite: Raan – Indian Roast Leg of Lamb (**page 24**) served on a large Naan Bread (**page 60**)

Firstly   Buy small quantities. Once they are opened, the spices deteriorate and eventually lose all their flavour (or essential oils). Use them within 6-12 months of opening for ground spices and 12-18 months for whole spices. Beyond those dates, bin them and buy fresh.

Secondly   Store in an airtight lidded container, in a dry place. Temperature is not important, but it is better cooler rather than hotter.

Thirdly   Do not be tempted to display your spices in alluring glass jars. Ultraviolet and especially direct sunlight fades the colours and, more important the tastes. Spices are best kept in a dark place – a cupboard or pantry.

THE SPICES YOU NEED

The following list will enable you to make all the dishes in this book; an asterisk indicates that the particular spice is used in only one or two recipes. The Hindi/Urdu words follow in brackets.

Whole Spices

anise, star (saunf star)   *
bay leaves (tej patia)
cardamom black/brown (elaichi burra)
cardamom white/green (elaichi chota)
cassia bark (dalchini)
chillies whole, red, dried (lal mirch)
cloves (lavang)
coriander seeds (dhania)
cummin seeds, black (kala jeera)   *
cummin seeds, white (jeera)
fennel seeds (soonf)
fenugreek leaves, dried (tej methi)
fenugreek seeds (methi)   *
lovage seeds (ajwain or ajowan)   *

mustard seeds, black (kala rai)
onion seeds, wild (nigella or kalongi)
peppercorns, black (mirch)
poppy seeds, white (cuscus)
sesame seeds, white (til)

Ground Spices

Some spices are best bought as factory ground spices:

chilli powder (lal mirch)
coriander (dhania)
cummin (jeera)
mango powder (am chur)   *
paprika
pepper, black (mirch)
turmeric (huldi)

ROASTING SPICES

Some recipes in this book call for roasted spices. This is easy and it's fun and the results you get are stupendous. The analogy is coffee. The 'roasting' process releases those delicious aromatic fragrances, the essential oils, into the air.

The simplest way to 'roast' spices is to putthem into a pre-heated dry frying pan or wok which you put on a medium heat on the stove. Dry stir-fry (no oil or water, remember) for 30-60 seconds to release the aromas. Do not let the spices burn, and if theydo then bin them – it's cheap enough and quick enough to start again. Cool the spices. You can store them, but it is better to roast them and use them immediately as required.

GRINDING SPICES

Roast them first and cool them. Then grind in a mortar and pestle if you enjoy hard work, or in a coffee grinder or spice mill.

GARAM MASALA

— ◆ —

This is the best example of roasting and grinding your own spices. Try it, at least once, please. Then compare it with any brand of factory-made garam masala. I guarantee you'll do-it-yourself from then on.

Garam means hot; masala, mixture of spices. The heat comes from the pepper. There are as many mixtures as there are cooks but all should use aromatic spices. Here is a particularly aromatic version, suitable for tandoori dishes. Next time you may wish to add other spices or make other changes.

Garam masala is best used towards the end of the cooking. Add it too early, and you lose its aromatic qualities. It can also be sprinkled over a finished dish as a garnish. I've used metric weights only. Tablespoons (heaped) are acceptable but less accurate.

Makes: 175 g (about 11 heaped tablespoons when ground)

50 g (8 heaped tablespoons) coriander seeds	*15 g (2 heaped tablespoons) fennel seeds*
40 g (4 heaped tablespoons) cummin seeds	*10 g (2 heaped tablespoons) cloves*
20 g (2 heaped tablespoons) black peppercorns	*10 g (1 heaped tablespoon) green cardamom seeds*
20 g (several pieces) cassia bark	*7 g (several) bay leaves, dried*
	3 g (1 teaspoon) wild onion seeds

Lightly roast everything under a low-medium grill or in a low oven. Do not let the spices burn. They should give off a light steam. When they give off an aroma, remove from the heat, cool and grind in batches.

After grinding, mix thoroughly and store in an airtight jar. Garam masala will last almost indefinitely, but it is always better to make small batches every few months to get the best flavours.

DRY GROUND SPICE MASALA MIXTURES

Many of the recipes in this book require curry or tandoori pastes. These can be purchased bottled. The Curry Club makes an excellent range, but you may enjoy the challenge of making your own. It is not at all hard, requiring just a little of your time. To make home made bottled pastes, it is first necessary to make up a mixture of dry spices.

MILD CURRY MASALA (DRY MIXTURE)

— ◆ —

You could use commercially blended curry powder, but here is an alternative and very aromatic do-it-yourself version.

It is better to weigh the spices, though they do vary from batch to batch in density and water content. Tablespoon measures can be used but with less accuracy. This blend will mature and improve if left for a while before using, but it should be used within 6 months.

Makes: 265 g (about 17 tablespoons when ground)

WHOLE SPICES
100 g (16 tablespoons) coriander seeds
40 g (4¹/₂ tablespoons) white cummin seed
15 g (2 tablespoons) fennel seeds
15 g (2 tablespoons) fenugreek seeds
15 g (several pieces) cassia bark
15 g (2 tablespoons) cloves
5 g (several) bay leaves

GROUND SPICES
25 g (1³/₄ tablespoons) garam masala (page 4)
25 g (1³/₄ tablespoons) turmeric
10 g (²/₃ tablespoon) ginger

Roast and grind the whole spices, then blend with the ground spices and store.

TANDOORI MASALA
(DRY MIXTURE)

— ◆ —

As with all pre-mixed masalas, this has the advantage of maturing during storage. Keep it in the dark in an airtight container and it will be good for 6-12 months.

Makes: 265 g (about 17 tablespoons)

40 g (8 teaspoons) ground
 coriander

35 g (7 teaspoons) ground
 cummin

35 g (7 teaspoons) garlic
 powder

35 g (7 teaspoons) paprika

25 g (5 teaspoons) ground
 ginger

25 g (5 teaspoons) mango
 powder

5 g (2 teaspoons) dried mint

25 g (5 teaspoons) beetroot
 powder (deep red
 colouring)   *

10 g (2 teaspoons) chilli
 powder

10 g (2 teaspoons) anatto
 seed powder (yellow
 colouring)   *

Simply mix the ingredients together well and store. Use as described in the recipes.

Note: *You can use food colouring powder instead but use only 5 g red and 3 g sunset yellow. These small quantities will achieve a more vibrant colour than beetroot and anatto.

FRYING GROUND SPICES

Factory ground spices are not roasted first (and that includes factory packaged garam masala). Consequently, unless you cook them before use their essential oils will not be released and they will taste raw, no matter what you do. To cook them, mix the ground spice – usually more than one spice – with an equal volume of water to make a paste. Fry that paste in oil to remove the water. The rawness is cooked out and the paste can be incorporated into subsequent cooking.

MILD CURRY PASTE

— ◆ —

This mild paste can form the base for many curry dishes. Using vinegar (rather than all water) to make the paste will enable you to preserve it in jars. As with pickling, sterilise the jars (a good hot wash in the dishwasher followed by a dry-out in a low-heat oven will do). Top off the paste in the jar with hot oil and inspect after a few days to see that there is no mould. If there is, carefully scrape off the surface mould and re-cook the paste with some more vinegar.

Makes: about 1¹/₂ lb (675 g)

1 *full recipe mild curry*	6-8 *fl oz (175-250 ml)*
masala (page 5)	*vegetable oil*
6-8 *fl oz (175-250 ml)*	
vinegar (any type)	

Mix the curry powder spices with the vinegar and enough water to make a creamy paste. Heat the oil in a karahi or wok, then add the paste to the oil – it will splutter a bit, so be careful. Stir-fry continually to prevent it sticking until the water content is cooked out (it should take 5 minutes).

As the liquid is reduced, the paste will begin to make a regular bubbling noise (hard to describe, but it goes chup, chup, chup, chup) if you don't stir, and it will splatter. This is your audible cue that it is ready. You can tell if the spices are cooked by taking the karahi off the stove. Leave to stand for 3-4 minutes. If the oil 'floats' to the top, the spices are cooked. If not, add a little more oil and repeat. Bottle the paste in sterilised jars. Then heat up a little more oil and 'cap' off the paste by pouring in enough oil to cover. Seal the jars and store.

GREEN MASALA PASTE

— ◆ —

This curry paste is green in colour because of its use of coriander and mint. You can buy it factory made, but it does not have the delicious fresh taste of this recipe from Ivan Watson, journalist and regular correspondent of *The Curry Magazine*. You will come across green masala paste in the Indian home where it is used to enhance curry dishes and impart a subtle flavour that can be obtained in no other way. As with all curry pastes, this one will keep in jars indefinitely if made correctly.

Makes: about 1 lb (450 g)

1 teaspoon fenugreek seeds
6 garlic cloves, chopped
2 tablespoons finely chopped freh ginger
1¹/₂ oz (40 g) fresh mint leaves
1¹/₂ oz (40 g) fresh coriander leaves
4 fl oz (100 ml) vinegar, (any type)

3 teaspoons salt
3 teaspoons turmeric
2 teaspoons chilli powder
¹/₂ teaspoon ground cloves
1 teaspoon ground cardamom seeds
4 fl oz (100 ml) vegetable oil
2 fl oz (50 ml) sesame oil

Soak the fenugreek seeds in water overnight. They will swell and acquire a jelly-like coating. Strain the fenugreek, discarding the water. Mulch down all the ingredients, except the oils, in a blender or food processor, to make a purée. Heat the two oils in a karahi or wok and cook the purée by following the curry paste method on pages 7-8.

RED TANDOORI PASTE

— ◆ —

Most restaurants use bright red tandoori paste to colour and spice their marinade. It is not difficult to make your own.

Makes: about 1¹/₂ lb (675 g)

1 full recipe tandoori masala　　*6-8 fl oz (175 to 250 ml)*
　dry mixture (page 6)　　　　*vegetable oil*
6-8 fl oz (175 to 250 ml)
　vinegar (any type)

Mix the tandoori masala spices with the vinegar and enough water to make a creamy paste. Heat the oil in a karahi or wok and cook the purée following the curry paste method on pages 7-8.

MARINATION

The longer you marinate meat or poultry, the better will be the penetration of the marinade. Storage of raw meat and poultry requires great care. If it has been once frozen then thawed, it will be acceptable to marinate in the fridge for up to 24 hours and no more. If the meat or poultry is fresh and has come straight from the vendor's fridge to your own, providing you stay within the 'use by' date, if applicable, it will be acceptable to marinate up to 60 hours in the fridge. Any marination, even after 24 hours, should be thoroughly inspected and smelt. The meat or poultry should look firm and smell clean. Longer marinations are successful using the freezer, but not if the meat or poultry has already been frozen.

Fish and shellfish can also be marinaded but require much less time in the marinade than meat or poultry.

On pages 11-13 are three different tandoori marinades. To ring the changes, if you wish, you can substitute any one of them for any other in recipes in this book which call for tandoori marinades.

RED TANDOORI MARINADE

— ◆ —

Yoghurt, oil, lemon juice and a little milk are used to 'suspend' the spices for this red tandoori marinade.

Makes: about 14 oz (400 g) marinade

5 oz (150 g) plain yoghurt
2 tablespoons vegetable oil
2 tablespoons bottled or
  fresh lemon juice
2 or 3 garlic cloves, chopped
2 or 3 fresh red chillies,
  chopped (optional)
2 tablespoons chopped fresh
  coriander leaves
1 teaspoon cummin seeds,
  roasted and ground

1 teaspoon garam masala
1 teaspoon mild curry paste
  (page 5)
2 tablespoons red tandoori
  paste (page 9)
1 tablespoon tomato purée
1/2 teaspoon salt
about 4 fl oz (100 ml) milk
  (maybe more, maybe less)

Put the yoghurt, oil, lemon juice, garlic, chillies and fresh coriander leaves into the blender and pulse it into as fine a purée as you can get. Add all the remaining ingredients except the milk and continue pulsing. Now add milk until the purée is easy to pour. As there are some variables in the ingredients you may need more or less milk than stated. The colour should be creamy scarlet. Refrigerate until needed.

Note: Some recipes require about 7 oz (200 g) of marinade. Simply halve the above quantities.

GREEN TANDOORI MARINADE

— ◆ —

Green tandoori dishes are not traditional but I've been using gorgeous herby natural colour marinades for years to achieve fine tandoori-style results.

Makes: about 14 oz (400 g) marinade

5 oz (150 g) plain yoghurt
2 tablespoons vegetable oil
2 tablespoons bottled or
    fresh lemon juice
3 or 4 garlic cloves, chopped
2 or 3 fresh green chillies,
    chopped (optional)
3 tablespoons chopped fresh
    mint leaves
3 tablespoons chopped fresh
    coriander leaves

3 tablespoons green masala
    paste (page 8)
1 teaspoon cummin seeds,
    roasted and ground
1 teaspoon garam masala
1/2 teaspoon salt
about 4 fl oz (100 ml) milk
    (maybe more, maybe less)

Put the yoghurt, oil, lemon juice, garlic, chillies, leaves and paste into the blender and pulse it into as fine a paste as you can. Add all the remaining ingredients except the milk and continue pulsing. Now add enough milk to make the purée easy to pour. As there are some variables in the ingredients you may need more or less milk than stated. The colour should be creamy dark green. Refrigerate until needed.

Note: Some recipes require about 7 oz (200 g) of marinade. Simply halve the above quantities.

RAAN OR AROMATIC
TANDOORI MARINADE

— ◆ —

This marinade is, perhaps, even more unusual than the previous green one. It is another of my modifications to the traditional red tandoori marinade which concentrates on aromatics rather than colour. It was devised for *raan* (see page 24) but it works admirably for all dishes. Its colour, by the way, is neutral creamy buff, but this cooks into a gorgeous brown crispy finish.

Makes: about 14 oz (400 g) marinade

5 oz (150 g) plain yoghurt
2 tablespoons sesame or mustard blend oil
2 tablespoons bottled or fresh lemon juice
3 or 4 garlic cloves, chopped
1 inch (2.5 cm) cube fresh ginger
2 or 3 fresh green chillies, chopped
1 tablespoon chopped fresh coriander leaves
4 tablespoons dried onion flakes

2 tablespoons ground almonds
¹/₂ teaspoon salt
about 4 fl oz (100 ml) milk (maybe more, maybe less)

SPICES (roasted and ground)
2 tablespoons coriander seeds
1 tablespoon sesame seeds
1 teaspoon green cardamom seeds
1 teaspoon fennel seeds

Put the yoghurt, oil, lemon juice, garlic, ginger, chillies and leaves into the blender and pulse it into as fine a paste as you can. Add all the remaining ingredients, including the spices, and pulse until you get a purée which is easy to pour. You will almost certainly need a little more milk than the measured amount, but add it little by little. Refrigerate until needed.

Note: Some recipes require approximately 7 oz (200 g) of marinade. Simply halve the above quantities.

TIKKA/TANDOORI MASALA CURRY GRAVY

— ◆ —

Tikka/tandoori masala gravy is a relatively recent UK curry house invention, which has become so popular that it is even to be found on the menus of the better restaurants in Bombay and Delhi. It is a curry master sauce or gravy which is spiced in the tandoori style and should be a gorgeous reddish colour. It can be used in its own right, or it can be used to make dryish tikka/tandoori dishes into tikka masala curries – for example, the recipes on pages 28 and 41–3.

Makes: about 16 oz (450 g) gravy, sufficient for 2 tikka masala curry portions

2 tablespoons vegetable oil
2 garlic cloves, minced
4 oz (110 g) onion, very finely chopped
1 tablespoon mild curry paste (page 7)
1-2 tablespoons red tandoori paste (page 9)
4 canned plum tomatoes
1 tablespoon vinegar
1 tablespoon tomato ketchup
6 fl oz (175 ml) canned tomato soup

$^{1}/_{2}$ green capsicum pepper, chopped
0-4 green chillies (optional)
3 fl oz (75 ml) single cream
2 tablespoons coconut milk powder (optional)
1 tablespoon garam masala
1 tablespoon dried fenugreek leaf
1 tablespoon chopped fresh coriander
salt to taste

Heat the oil in a large karahi or wok. Stir-fry the garlic for 30 seconds, then add the onion and stir-fry for 8-10 minutes. Add the pastes and stir-fry for a couple of minutes. Add the tomatoes, vinegar, ketchup, soup, capsicum and chillies. Simmer and stir-fry for 5 minutes or so then add the remaining ingredients and simmer for a further 5 minutes, adding water as needed to maintain a gravy consistency. Salt to taste and serve.

SIZZLERS

Tandoori and tikka dishes can be served to the table very hot, smoking and sizzling like a rocket going into space. This is a restaurant technique and to do it you'll need to buy special heavy steel sizzlers (see page vi for mail order address). There are two types – a flat oval tray and a small two-handled karahi dish, each made of cast iron and each with a wooden base. They make an attractive presentation, but be careful not to burn yourself, your guests or your table with the excruciatingly fire-hot dishes, nor to splutter hot oil over their clothes.

Any of the dry tandoori and tikka recipes in this book can be served sizzling. The technique is simple when you know how. The food is cooked to readiness in a separate pan. Just prior to serving, place the dry cast-iron pan directly on to the stove over a ring at its hottest. Let the metal get as hot as it can. It takes at least five minutes.

Add a teaspoon or two of ghee or oil to the pan and turn off the heat (so the oil doesn't catch fire).

Carefully add ½ teaspoon water or lime juice. Take care, because the hot oil and water will splutter and steam. Add the food at once. Do not load the pan over half full or you may lose the effect. Take to the table still hissing.

Remember: The pan is blisteringly hot, though still innocently black, so use oven gloves and treat it all with respect!

SALAD BEDS

Many of the tikka and tandoori dishes in this book can be served on a bed of salad – but this need not be just a bed of lettuce. Here are some possibilities. Salad vegetables are not only good for you – they give a dish a fresh look with excellent colour contrasts. Buy fresh and use on the same day for best appearance.

Choose from a combination of the following and place

artistically on your serving dish. Place the main dish on top, and garnish with mustard and cress and lemon and lime wedges.

Shredded
iceburg lettuce, Chinese leaf, endive top, radicchio, spinach, white cabbage

Strips
red, green, yellow, black capsicum pepper, carrot, white radish (mooli), chillies, fresh coconut

Leaf
coriander, whole, chopped or shredded, stalks removed, parsley, dill, fennel, watercress

GARNISHES

Any of the above vegetables can be used to garnish curry dishes just prior to serving, improving their appearance quite considerably. The following items can also be used:

Nuts - such as pistachio, almonds and cashew can be added whole or chopped, raw, 'roasted' or fried. Do not use salted nuts.

Onions – dried fried onion flakes are attractive and crunchy and can easily be bought ready to use.

Leafy herbs – can be used raw but for a fascinating change try deep-frying them (375°F/190°C). It only takes a few seconds. They whoosh and go dark green almost at once. Remove from the oil and drain on kitchen paper. They will go crispy quite soon. Then serve.

Cream – a curl of cream can look attractive.

Opposite (top to bottom): Tandoori Keema Naan (**page 62**), Tandoori Keema Masala Curry (**page 26**), and stuffed Tandoori Turkey Breast (**pages 37-8**) with a slice removed to reveal the stuffing, on a bed of Fried Pullao Rice (**page 59**)

Opposite page 17 (top to bottom): Squid Ring Tikka (**page 42**), Tandoori Snapper (**page 45**).

CHAPTER 2

Meat

Ancient tribesmen first marinated their meat, from animals they caught in the wild, to tenderise it. The added bonus was and is the superlative spicy flavours that penetrate it.

For best results with all these recipes use top quality meat.

TANDOORI LAMB CHOP

— ◆ —

Chops and ribs are ideal for barbecuing and can be eaten with the fingers.

Serves: 2 as part of the main course, or 4 as a starter

8 lamb chops, about 4 oz (115 g) each   *14 oz (400 g) red tandoori marinade (page 11)*

Remove some but not all of the fat from the chops and prick the meat all over with a fork. Coat the chops in the marinade in a non-metallic bowl. Cover and put into the fridge for 24 to 60 hours (see page 10).

To cook, preheat the grill to high heat. Put the chops on a foil-lined grill tray and place this in the midway position under the heat. Alternatively they can be barbecued. Cook for about 8 minutes, then turn over and cook for a further 8 minutes or so. Serve on a bed of salad with lemon wedges, naan bread and tandoori chutney.

MEAT TIKKA

— ◆ —

Best quality meat gives best results. When cooked, it should be tender yet slightly chewy, like a good steak. Use any lean filleted meat – beef, pork, venison or veal. The traditional meat is lamb.

Serves: 2 as a starter

7 oz (200 g) red tandoori marinade (page 11)

8-10 chunky pieces lean meat, cut into 1½ inch (4 cm) cubes

Mix the marinade ingredients in a large non-metallic bowl. Place the cubes of meat into the marinade, ensuring that they are well coated. Cover the bowl and refrigerate for 24 hours minimum, 60 hours maximum (see page 10).

When ready to cook, preheat oven to 425°F/220°C/Gas 7. Line an oven tray with foil and place the oven rack above the tray. Remove the meat from the marinade and thread the cubes on to two skewers, leaving a little space between each chunk (this helps heat transference). Place the skewers on the oven rack and cook for 15-20 minutes, depending on your oven. A degree of pinkness or rareness in the middle of the meat may be preferred, and this is acceptable – adjust cooking times accordingly. Serve on a bed of salad with lemon wedges and tandoori chutney.

TANDOORI MIXED GRILL

— ◆ —

One of the restaurants' favourite presentations is the tandoori/tikka mixed grill. You can create your own mixed grill by choosing a selection of recipes from this chapter. Adjust quantities to suit the number of people you are serving. It's ideal for parties and barbecues – your imagination is already working overtime!

TANDOORI STEAK

— ◆ —

Use any type of steak such as sirloin, entrêcote, fillet or rump.

Serves: 4 as a main course

4 steaks, each weighing 6-8 oz (175-225 g)

14 oz (400 g) red, green or raan tandoori marinade (page 13)

Prick the steaks with a fork and coat thoroughly with the marinade in a non-metallic bowl. Cover and put in the fridge for 24 hours minimum, 60 hours maximum (see page 10).

To cook, preheat the grill to high heat. Put the steaks on to a rack above a foil-lined grill tray and place this in the midway position under the heat. Alternatively, they can be barbecued. Cook for about 4 minutes, turning at least once, for rare steaks; longer for medium etc. To finish off, raise the tray nearer to the heat and singe the steaks to obtain a little blackening. Serve on a bed of salad with lemon wedges, naan bread and tandoori chutney.

TIKKA RIBS
(PORK CHOPS)

— ◆ —

Serve these finger-licking ribs as part of a tandoori mixed grill (see page 18) or even as a starter.

Serves: 2 as part of a main course, or 4 as a starter

16 tiny barbecue pork ribs,   *7 oz (200 g) red tandoori*
   each weighing 1 oz (25 g),   *marinade (page 11)*
   or 12 larger ones

Prick the meat with a fork and coat the ribs in the marinade in a non-metallic bowl. Cover and put into the fridge for 24 hours minimum, 60 hours maximum (see page 10).

To cook, preheat the grill to high heat. Put the ribs on a rack above a foil-lined grill tray and place this in the midway position under the heat. Alternatively they can be barbecued. Cook for about 5 minutes for tiny ribs, a bit longer for larger ribs. Turn and cook for a further few minutes. Serve on a bed of salad with lemon wedges, naan bread and tandoori chutney.

SHEEK KEBABS

— ◆ —

You can use cheaper cuts of meat, but you won't get better kebabs than with fillet steak.

Serves: 4 as part of a main course, or 2 as a starter

1^1/$_2$ lb (675 g) fillet steak, weighed after discarding fat and unwanted matter

1 tablespoon dried onion flakes

2 garlic cloves, finely chopped

0-4 fresh green chillies, chopped

1 tablespoon red tandoori paste (page 9)

1 tablespoon garam masala

1 tablespoon chopped fresh mint

1 tablespoon chopped fresh coriander

1 teaspoon salt

Chop the meat into strips, discarding any unwanted matter. Run it through a hand or electric mincer two or three times until it is lump free and finely ground. In a large bowl mix all the ingredients together by hand. The mixture should be fairly sticky.

Clean your hands before and frequently during this stage. Divide the mixture into four. Make it into four sausage shapes and slip these on to skewers.

To cook, preheat the grill to high heat. Put the skewers on to a rack above a foil-lined grill tray and place this in the midway position under the heat. Alternatively, they can be barbecued. Cook for 8-10 minutes, turning at least once. To finish off, raise the tray nearer to the heat and singe the kebabs to obtain a little blackening. Serve on a bed of salad with lemon wedges, naan bread and tandoori chutney.

TANDOORI HARE (OR RABBIT)

— ◆ —

Not encountered in the average tandoori house, perhaps, but an excellent subject for this style of cooking, being the ideal size and good flavour. One 5 lb (2.25 kg) skinned hare or rabbit will yield about 1¼ lb (560 g) meat. Keep it on the bone, but get it jointed into legs and back pieces.

Serves: 4 as a starter

6 or 8 hare or rabbit pieces, skinned and on the bone	14 oz (400 g) red tandoori marinade (page 11)

Prick the meat with a fork and coat thoroughly with the marinade in a non-metallic bowl. Cover and put in the fridge for 24 hours minimum, 60 hours maximum (see page 10).

To cook, preheat the grill to medium heat. Put the meat pieces on to a rack above a foil-lined grill tray and place this in the midway position under the heat. Alternatively, they can be barbecued. Cook for 15-20 minutes, turning at least once. Test that the pieces are cooked to your liking. To finish off, raise the tray nearer to the heat and singe the meat pieces to obtain a little blackening. Serve on a bed of salad with lemon wedges, naan bread and tandoori chutney.

TANDOORI TURBAN CROWN ROAST OF LAMB

— ◆ —

Here's an invention of mine, or rather a modification of an old classic favourite. The meat is the ribs from the 'best end neck' of the lamb. Your butcher will remove unwanted matter and form the crown using at least 14 cutlet ribs, on top of which will be placed 'cutlet frills', which from now on we'll call 'turbans'. Tell him you want the crown plain, and 'without cap and filling', (some butchers fill the crown with fat taken from the ribs, but you don't want this). Ask for some spare turbans, in case!

Serves: 4

one 14-16 rib crown roast
14 oz (200 ml) raan tandoori
marinade (page 13)

STUFFING
8 oz (225 g) cooked plain
rice, cold

4 oz (110 g) fresh spinach,
shredded
2 tablespoons dried onion
flakes
1 tablespoon green masala
paste (page 8)

Remove and keep the 'turbans'. Weigh the crown before you start and make a note of it. Prick the cutlets with a fork and coat thoroughly with the marinade in a non-metallic bowl. Cover and put in the fridge for 24 hours minimum, 60 hours maximum (see page 10).

To cook, preheat the oven to 350°F/180°C/Gas 4. Mix the stuffing ingredients together. Carefully put the crown on to an oven tray, then pack the stuffing into the centre and spoon the excess marinade on top of the stuffing. Cap the stuffing with a shaped piece of foil and put the tray into the oven. Calculating cooking time from your noted weight, roast for 25 minutes per lb (450 g), plus 20 minutes. Baste at least twice with juices from the oven pan.

To serve, place the roast on to a warm serving dish. There should be some juices in the oven tray. Discard excess oil and pour the juices into the stuffing. Replace the turbans and serve with naan bread, vegetables and roast tikka potatoes (page 48).

RAAN – INDIAN ROAST LEG OF LAMB

— ◆ —

This is a traditional Indian dish devised centuries ago for the Moghul emperors and cooked in the clay oven. Cook it in the conventional oven very slowly until it is to your liking, or until it is so tender that the flesh just falls off the bone.

Serves: 4 as part of a main course

$3^{1}/_{2}$-4 lb (1.5-1.8 kg) leg of
   lamb on the bone
14 oz (400 g) raan tandoori
   marinade (page 13)

GARNISH
20-30 *whole raw almonds,*
   fried or lightly toasted
20-30 *whole fresh coriander*
   leaves

Pare away all fat and skin membrane from the meat. Stab it all over with a small knife and coat thoroughly with the marinade in a non-metallic bowl. Cover and put in the fridge for 24 hours minimum, 60 hours maximum (see page 10).

To cook, preheat the oven to 350°F/180°C/Gas 4 maximum. Transfer the lamb and marinade to a roasting dish and slow-roast for about 3 hours. When really tender the flesh should literally fall off the bone. Prior to serving, let it rest for 30 minutes or so in a low oven.

Garnish by covering with the almonds, then sprinkle with fresh coriander leaves. Serve with the gravy from the roasting pan and any sediment on the bottom of the pan. Accompany with roast tikka potatoes (page 48) and a vegetable dish from Chapter Five.

TANDOORI ROAST TOPSIDE OF BEEF

— ◆ —

A gorgeous modern variation of the previous classic, which makes a marvellous change for Sunday lunch.

Serves: 4-6

2¹/₂-3¹/₂ lb (1.1-1.5 kg) piece
of beef topside, weighed
after removing all fat and
membrane

14 oz (200 g) red tandoori
marinade (page 11)

Pare away all fat and skin membrane from the meat. Stab it all over with a small knife and coat thoroughly with the marinade in a non-metallic bowl. Cover and put in the fridge for 24 hours minimum, 60 hours maximum (see page 10).

To cook, preheat the oven to 350°F/180°C/Gas 4 maximum, and slow-roast the beef for about 2 hours, until really tender. Prior to serving, let it rest for 30 minutes or so in a low oven.

Serve with roast tikka potatoes (page 48) and a vegetable dish from Chapter Five.

TANDOORI KEEMA MASALA CURRY

— ◆ —

Minced beef is cheap and easy to cook. It is perfect for tandoori-style curry, as this recipe proves.

Serves: 4

1¹/₂ lb (675 g) lean minced beef	1 tablespoon tomato purée
3 tablespoons vegetable oil	1 tablespoon mango chutney, finely chopped
2 garlic cloves, very finely chopped	5 fl oz (150 ml) canned tomato soup
6 oz (175 g) onion, very finely chopped	¹/₂ red capsicum pepper, chopped
1 tablespoon mild curry paste (page 7)	1 tablespoon garam masala
1 tablespoon red tandoori paste (page 9)	4 fl oz (100 ml) single cream
6 cherry tomatoes, chopped	1 tablespoon chopped fresh coriander leaves
	salt to taste

Preheat the oven to 375°F/190°C/Gas 5. Heat the oil in a karahi or wok and add the garlic, onion and pastes. Stir-fry for 10 minutes. Add the mince and stir-fry for 5-10 minutes. Transfer it all to a 4¹/₂ pint (2.6 l) lidded casserole, adding the tomatoes, purée, chutney, soup and capsicum. Stir well, put on the lid and put the dish into the hot oven.

After about 20 minutes inspect, stir and add a little stock or water if needed. Continue to cook for another 20 minutes, then add the garam masala, cream and fresh coriander. Cook for at least 10 more minutes. Just prior to serving, spoon off any excess oil. Salt to taste and serve.

LAMB TIKKA MASALA CURRY

— ◆ —

A popular and tasty curry, well worth the effort to make it.

Serves: 4

20-24 pieces lamb tikka
   cooked to the recipe at top
   of page 18
3 tablespoons vegetable oil
4 garlic cloves, minced
8 oz (225 g) onions, very
   finely chopped
1 tablespoon mild curry
   paste (page 7)
2 tablespoons red tandoori
   paste (page 9)
1 tablespoon green masala
   paste (page 8)
6 canned plum tomatoes

2 tablespoons vinegar (any
   type)
1 tablespoon tomato ketchup
6 oz (175 g) canned tomato
   soup
$^1/_2$ green capsicum pepper,
   chopped
0-4 green chillies (optional)
4 fl oz (100 ml) single cream
1 tablespoon garam masala
1 tablespoon chopped fresh
   coriander
salt to taste

Heat the vegetable oil in a large karahi or wok. Stir-fry the garlic for 30 seconds, then add the onion and stir-fry for 8-10 minutes until golden brown. Add the pastes and stir-fry for a couple of minutes. Add the tomatoes, vinegar, ketchup, soup, capsicum and chillies, and when simmering add the lamb.

Stir-fry for 5 minutes or so, then add the remaining ingredients and simmer for a further 10 minutes, or until the meat is to your liking, adding water as needed to maintain a nice gravy consistency. Salt to taste and serve.

LIVER TIKKA

— ◆ —

Delicious for a change and very simply cooked as a stir-fry.

Serves: 4 as a starter

1 lb (450 g) lamb's liver,
　chopped into 1 inch (2.5
　cm) cubes
7 fl oz (200 ml) red tandoori
　marinade (page 11)

4 tablespoons ghee or
　vegetable oil
1 teaspoon cummin seeds
salt to taste

Note: Heart, brain or kidney can be substituted for liver, or a combination can be used.

In a non-metallic bowl, mix the liver with the marinade. Cover and refrigerate for 6 hours minimum, 24 hours maximum.

　To cook, heat the ghee or oil in a large karahi or wok. Add the cummin seeds, then the liver pieces, shaking off any excess marinade. Stir-fry for 5-8 minutes. Test that it is cooked by cutting through a piece. Salt to taste. Serve on a bed of salad with naån bread and lemon wedges.

LIVER TIKKA MASALA CURRY

Lamb Tikka can easily become a tikka or tandoori masala curry by adding it and any spare marinade to a full portion (16 oz/450 g) of cooked tikka/tandoori masala gravy (page 14). Cook the gravy first, and keep it warm or reheat it to coincide with the timing of your tikka ingredients.

CHAPTER · 3

— ◆ —

Poultry and Game

By far the most popular dishes on Indian restaurant menus are chicken, and Chicken Tikka Masala is probably the most popular of all (see page 38).

TANDOORI CHICKEN LEGS

— ◆ —

Use the entire leg – the thigh and the 'drumstick' (the joint below the knee and above the ankle).

2 chicken legs (see above)	*14 oz (200 g) red tandoori*
juice of 1 lemon	*marinade (page 11)*

Skin the legs, keeping each in one piece. Gash the flesh with the tip of a knife and rub in the lemon juice. Allow it to dry.

Mix the marinade and legs in a large non-metallic bowl. Cover and refrigerate for 24 to 60 hours (see page 10).

To cook, preheat the grill to medium heat. Put the legs on to a rack above a foil-lined grill tray and place this in the midway position under the heat. Alternatively, they can be barbecued. Cook for at least 10 minutes, turning at least once. Test by piercing the plumpest part of the leg. The fluid which runs out must be clear; if not, cook for longer.

To finish off, raise the tray nearer to the heat and singe the legs to obtain a little blackening. Serve on a bed of salad with lemon wedges, naan bread and tandoori chutney.

TANDOORI WHOLE CHICKEN

— ◆ —

For best results try to obtain a farm-fresh double poussin (a 6-10 week old young chicken) whose 'oven-ready' weight is 1¹/₂-2 lb (675-900 g).

Serves: 2 as a starter

1 double poussin (see above)	*7 oz (200 g) red tandoori*
juice of 2 lemons	*marinade (page 11)*

Remove and discard the skin and clean the chicken inside and out. With the tip of a sharp knife, make short gashes all over the flesh (this gives a greater surface area for the marinade). Rub all over with the lemon juice (this degreases it and makes the marinade penetrate better), then leave to dry for about 30 minutes.

Put the chicken in a large non-metallic bowl. Cover the chicken with the marinade, massaging it into the gashes. Cover the bowl and refrigerate for 24 to 60 hours (see page 10).

To cook, preheat the oven to 375°F/190°C/Gas 5. Place the chicken on a skewer lengthwise, and place at the top of the oven. Put a tray lined with foil underneath to catch the drips. Cook for 20 minutes,then turn over. Continue to cook for 20-30 more minutes, until cooked through. When the leg is pricked clear liquid should run out. Serve with salad, onion rings, lemon wedges, naan bread (page 60) and tandoori chutney (pages 57-8).

TANDOORI BHARE MURGH

— ◆ —

Whole stuffed and roasted chicken. Also known as *kurzi*, the result should be crispy and dry, and spicy and mouth-watering. Serve with roast tikka potatoes (page 48).

Serves: 4 as a main course

3¹/₂-3³/₄ lb (1.5 kg-1.75 kg)
  roasting chicken
juice of 3 lemons
14 oz (400 ml) red tandoori
  marinade (page 11)
6 tablespoons ghee or
  vegetable oil
4 garlic cloves, finely
  chopped
2 tablespoons chopped fresh
  coriander

STUFFING
8 oz (225 g) cooked Basmati
  rice

4 oz (110 g) frozen mixed
  vegetable, thawed
4 fl oz (100 ml) Greek
  yoghurt
¹/₄ teaspoon salt

SPICES
1 teaspoon white cummin
  seeds
1 teaspoon coriander seeds
¹/₂ teaspoon black
  peppercorns
¹/₂ teaspoon black cummin
  seeds
¹/₂ teaspoon turmeric

Skin the chicken and clean it inside and out. Gash the flesh with the tip of a sharp knife and rub with the lemon juice to degrease it. Leave to dry for 30 minutes.

In a large non-metallic bowl, work the marinade well into the chicken. Cover and refrigerate for 24 hours minimum, 60 hours maximum (see page 10).

Heat the ghee or oil in large karahi or wok. Carefully place the chicken in and fry until all sides are browned (about 15 minutes). Remove from the pan, leaving the ghee and any cooked marinade behind. Mix together the stuffing ingredients. When the chicken is cold enough, stuff with the mixture.

Preheat the oven to 400°F/200°C/Gas 6. Fry the garlic in the pan, add the **spices**, the remaining cooked marinade and salt to taste, and simmer gently. Add ¹/₄ pint (150 ml) water bit by bit over 10 minutes. Put the chicken on its back in a large lidded casserole dish and pour the fried blend over it. Put on the lid, and place in the hot oven. Cook for about an hour, basting once or twice. Sprinkle the fresh coriander over the chicken, then cook without the lid for a minimum of 10 minutes. You'll probably need longer, and possibly an increase in heat to crust and dry the chicken – it's up to you, but keep a close eye on it. Strain off any spare oil (keep for future use).

TANDOORI WHOLE DUCK

— ◆ —

This is a variation of the previous recipe. Use a duckling of about 3-1//2 lb (1.5 kg) for two people as it yields less meat than chicken. Also you can use a different flavoured marinade if you wish.

Serves: 2 as a starter

3¹/₂ lb (1.5 kg) duckling	14 oz (400 g) raan tandoori
juice of 2 lemons	marinade (page 13)

Remove and discard the skin and clean the duckling inside and out. Poke a sharp knife deep into the duck all over then rub with lemon juice. Leave to dry for 30 minutes in a deep bowl. Discard any spare lemon juice.

Now work the marinade into the duck. Cover the bowl and refrigerate for 24 hours minimum, 60 hours maximum (see page 10).

To cook, preheat the oven to 350°F/180°C/Gas 4. Remove the duck from the bowl, shaking off any excess marinade, and place on an oven tray. Smear some of the excess marinade back on to the duck, enough to give it an even coating. Put the duck into the oven. The total roasting time will be about 1³/₄ hours (allowing 30 minutes per lb/450 g). After about 45 minutes, remove the duck and baste it with the remaining marinade. Return to the oven.

After 1¹/₂ hours, pierce the plump part of the leg. If it is cooked, the fluid that runs out will be clear; if not, cook for longer. The marinade will have caramelised into a fantastic crispy coating. Place the duck in a low oven to rest for 15 minutes, then cut into two servings, a half duck per person.

TANDOORI STUFFED AND GLAZED QUAIL

— ◆ —

Any small game bird can be tandoori cooked with excellent results. This version uses quail but you can equally use snipe or squab (young pigeon) or the larger grouse, woodcock or partridge. The glaze makes it quite outstandingly tasty.

Serves: 2

2 quail, skinned
7 oz (200 g) red tandoori
  marinade (page 11)
4 oz (110 g) cooked plain
  rice, cold

3 tablespoons clear honey
1 tablespoon Worcester
  sauce

Clean the quails inside and out. Immerse them in the marinade in a non-metallic bowl, then cover and put in the fridge for 24 hours minimum, 60 hours maximum (see page 10).

To cook, pre-heat the oven to 375°F/190°C/Gas 5. Remove the quails from the marinade and mix a tablespoon or so of it with the rice. Cram the quails full of the rice to stuff them. Put them on to a foil-lined oven tray and spoon any surplus marinade over them. Roast for 10 minutes.

Heat the honey and Worcester sauce in a small pan to make the glaze. Cover the quails with the glaze and roast for a further 5-8 minutes. Serve on a bed of salad with lime wedges.

CHICKEN TIKKA PIECES

— ◆ —

One of the most popular and delicious tikka dishes. For the equally popular chicken tikka masala, see page 38.

Serves: 2 as a starter

12 oz (375 g) chicken breast
 meat, skinned, filleted and
 cut into 1¹/₂ inch (4 cm)
 cubes

7 oz (200 g) red tandoori
 marinade (page 11)

Place the chicken and marinade in a non-metallic bowl. Cover and refrigerate for 24 to 60 hours (see page 10).

Just prior to cooking, thread the chicken pieces on to two skewers. (Use any spare marinade in a curry.) Preheat the grill to medium. Place the skewers on a rack above the foil-lined grill tray and place this in the midway position. Alternatively they can be barbecued. Cook for 5 minutes, turn and repeat. When fully cooked, raise the tray nearer to the heat and singe the pieces to obtain a little blackening. Serve on a bed of salad with lemon wedges, naan bread and tandoori chutney.

GREEN TANDOORI CHICKEN TIKKA

— ◆ —

This is an exciting variation of the previous (red) chicken tikka recipe, using this gorgeous herby green marinade.

Serves: 2

12 oz (375 g) chicken breast
 fillet, skinned, and cut into
 1¹/₂ inch (4 cm) cubes

7 oz (200 g) green tandoori
 marinade (page 12)

Follow exactly the method of the previous recipe.

DUCK TIKKA PIECES

— ◆ —

Duck breast makes excellent tikka. In this variation of the previous two recipes, we use raan marinade. You can, of course, use red or green alternatively.

Serves: 2

8-10 pieces duck breast,
  skinned, filleted and cut
  into 1½ inch (4 cm) cubes

7 oz (200 g) raan tandoori
  marinade (page 13)

Follow exactly the method of the recipe opposite.

TANDOORI DUCK BREAST

— ◆ —

Obtain top-quality filleted duck breasts. Magret de Canard are best. They will be supplied with a fatty layer of skin which must be removed before marinating.

Serves: 2 as a main course

2 skinless duck breasts, each
  weighing 6-8 oz (175-225 g)
  after the fat is removed

7 oz (200 g) red tandoori
  marinade (see page 11)

Slash the duck breasts with a knife, place in a non-metallic bowl and coat thoroughly with the marinade. Cover and refrigerate for 24 to 60 hours (see page 10).
  To cook, preheat the grill to high heat. Put the breasts on to a rack above a foil-lined grill tray and place this in the midway position. Alternatively, they can be barbecued. Cook for 6-8 minutes, turning at least once. To finish off raise nearer to the heat to blacken a little.

CHICKEN MAKHANWALLA

—— ◆ ——

A whole chicken is tandooried, then jointed and finished off in a tasty spicy red gravy topped with a butter tarka, the *makhanwalla*.

Serves: 4 as part of the main course

1 × 3½-3¾ lb (1.5-1.75 kg)
  roasting chicken
juice of 3 lemons
20 oz (600 g) red tandoori
  marinade (page 11)
2 tablespoons butter ghee
4 garlic cloves, finely
  chopped
8 oz (225 g) onion, very
  finely chopped
1 tablespoon mild curry
  paste (page 7)
2 tablespoons red tandoori
  paste (page 9)
8 canned plum tomatoes
6 fl oz (150 ml) canned
  tomato soup
1 tablespoon tomato purée

TARKA
3 tablespoons butter
2 tablespoons dried onion
  flakes
1 tablespoon garam masala
1 tablespoon chopped fresh
  coriander leaves
2 fresh red chillies chopped
  (optional)

SPICES
1 teaspoon cummin seeds
½ teaspoon fennel seeds
½ teaspoon cardamom seeds

GARNISH
a curl of single cream
roasted almond flakes
whole fresh coriander leaves
  and/or shredded fresh mint
  leaves

Skin the chicken, clean it inside and out and gash the flesh with the tip of a sharp knife. Rub it all over with the lemon juice and leave to dry for 30 minutes. In a large non-metallic bowl combine the chicken and marinade. Cover and refrigerate for 24 to 60 hours (see page 10).

To cook, pre-heat the oven to 350°F/180°C/Gas 4. Shake off and keep the considerable excess marinade and put the chicken into a large casserole dish. Put it into the oven without the lid and bake for 30 minutes. During this time, heat the ghee in a karahi and stir-fry the **spices** for 30 seconds. Add the garlic, and 30 seconds later add the onions, then reduce the heat and stir-fry for 15 minutes or so. Add the pastes and stir them in for a couple of minutes, then add the tomatoes, canned soup and purée and the excess marinade. Simmer for at least 15 minutes. Remove the chicken from the oven and joint it into 8 pieces (2 thighs, 2 drumsticks, 2 wings and 2 back pieces).

Return these pieces to the casserole with the simmering sauce and mix well. Put on the lid and bake for 20 minutes. In the karahi, heat the butter and stir-fry the tarka ingredients for 2-3 minutes, then place them on top of the chicken and cook for a final 10-20 minutes with the lid off. Salt to taste, garnish and serve.

STUFFED TANDOORI TURKEY

— ◆ —

This combination of spicy ground kebab beef inserted into tandoori marinated turkey is a winner.

Serves: 2 as part of a main course

2 × 6 oz (175 g) pieces turkey breast or thigh, skinned and filleted	4 oz (110 g) uncooked sheek kebab mix (page 21)
14 oz (200 g) raan tandoori marinade (page 13)	

Carefully cut a pocket in each turkey piece. Insert half the kebab mixture into each slit. Put the two pieces in a non-metallic bowl and coat thoroughly with the marinade. Cover and put in the fridge for 24 hours minimum, 60 hours maximum (see page 10).

To cook, preheat the grill to high heat. Put the pieces on a rack above a foil-lined grill tray and place this in the midway position under the heat. Alternatively, they can be barbecued. Cook for 15-20 minutes, turning at least once. To finish off, raise the tray nearer to the heat and singe the turkey pieces to obtain a little blackening. Cut the pieces crosswise into 6 or 7 slices each and serve with rice and a vegetable dish.

CHICKEN TIKKA MASALA

—— ◆ ——

At the tandoori restaurant, chicken is by far the most popular main ingredient, and chicken tikka masala, a pure restaurant invention (and a brilliant one), is by far the most popular restaurant dish.

Serves: 2-3

20-24 *chicken tikka pieces,*
  cooked to the recipe on
  page 34
2 *tablespoons vegetable oil*
3 *garlic cloves, minced*
8 *oz (225 g) onion, very*
  finely chopped
1¹/₂ *tablespoons mild curry*
  paste (page 7)
1¹/₂ *tablespoons red tandoori*
  paste (page 9)
1 *tablespoon green masala*
  paste (page 8)
6 *canned plum tomatoes*

1 *tablespoon vinegar (any*
  type)
1 *tablespoon tomato ketchup*
6 *fl oz (175 ml) canned*
  tomato soup
¹/₂ *green capsicum pepper,*
  chopped
0-4 *green chillies (optional)*
4 *fl oz (100 ml) single cream*
1 *tablespoon garam masala*
1 *tablespoon chopped fresh*
  coriander
salt to taste

Heat the oil in a large karahi or wok. Stir-fry the garlic for 30 seconds, then add the onion and stir-fry for 8-10 minutes, until golden brown. Add the pastes and stir-fry for a couple of minutes. Add the tomatoes, vinegar, ketchup, soup, capsicum and chillies, and when simmering add the chicken. Stir-fry for 5 minutes or so, then add the remaining ingredients and simmer for a further 5 minutes, adding a little water if it needs it. Salt to taste and serve.

CHAPTER · 4

Seafood

Though not traditionally found in the authentic tandoori cooking of the ancients, fish and shellfish adapt very well to the process. Marination times are much shorter than those of meat and poultry.

TANDOORI SKATE

— ◆ —

Serves: 4 as a starter

1¹/₂ lb-2 lb (700-900 g) wing
  of skate
juice of 2 lemons
1 teaspoon salt

¹/₂ teaspoon turmeric
7 oz (200 g) red tandoori
  marinade (page 11)
4 lemon wedges

Wash and dry the fish wing but keep it in one piece. Mix the lemon juice, salt and turmeric together, then rub it into the fish. Leave to stand for 30 minutes. Shake off any excess and coat the fish with the red marinade. Again let it stand for 30-60 minutes.

To cook, preheat the grill to medium heat. Put the skate on to a rack above a foil-lined grill tray and place this in the midway position under the heat. Alternatively, it can be barbecued. Cook for about 12-15 minutes, turning at least once. To finish off, raise the tray nearer to the heat and singe the skate to obtain a little blackening. Cut into four and serve with lemon wedges.

CRAB TIKKA

— ◆ —

Crab is very rarely seen at the tandoori house, which is a pity because, in this recipe, it is simple to cook and simply delicious! It's rich though, so a little goes a long way.

Serves: 2 as a starter

3 oz (75 g) fresh (or frozen)
  shredded white crab meat
1 oz (25 g) fresh (or frozen)
  shredded brown crab meat
1 tablespoon red tandoori
  paste (page 9)

3 or 4 tablespoons double
  cream
salt to taste
2 or 3 lemon wedges

Simply mix the crab, paste and cream together in a bowl. You can serve it hot or cold. If hot stir-fry it in a small frying pan until it's hot. If serving cold, refrigerate it for an hour or so. Whichever way you serve it, salt to taste and serve with salad and the lemon wedges.

CRAB TIKKA AVOCADO

Serves: 4 as a starter

Simply halve two avocados, dispose of the stones and fill the holes with the hot crab tikka, covering the whole top face of the avocado. Optionally cover with mozarella cheese and 'flash' the avocados under the grill until the cheese melts.

TIKKA COD CHUNKS

— ◆ —

The white filleted chunks look superb with the red marinade and taste just as good. Monkfish could be used instead.

Serves: 2 as a main course or 4 as a starter

12 oz (350 g) cod fillet
steaks, chopped into 1
inch (2.5 cm) cubes

7 oz (200 g) red tandoori
marinade (page 11)

In a non-metallic bowl, combine the fish chunks and the marinade and leave for up to 60 minutes.

To cook, preheat the grill to high heat. Slide the chunks on to four skewers, leaving a slight gap between each piece. Put the skewers on to a rack above a foil-lined grill tray and place this in the midway position under the heat. Alternatively, they can be barbecued. Cook for about 10 minutes, turning at least once. To finish off, raise the tray nearer to the heat to obtain a little blackening.

TIKKA KING PRAWN

— ◆ —

Here is a variation of the Tikka Cod Chunks recipe.

Serves: 4 as a starter or 2 as part of a main course

12 raw king prawns, each
weighing about 1 oz
(25-30 g) when thawed,
shelled, deveined and
cleaned

7 oz (200 g) green tandoori
marinade (page 12)

To prepare and cook, follow the previous recipe exactly.

SQUID RING TIKKA

— ◆ —

Another variation of the Tikka Cod Chunks recipe, this one making a superb crispy alternative to Spanish-style calemaries.

Serves: 2 as part of a main course

12 oz (350 g) pre-prepared
    squid, cleaned and cut into
    rings

7 oz (200 g) red tandoori
    marinade (page 11)

To prepare and cook, follow the Tikka Cod Chunks recipe on page 41 exactly.

LOBSTER TANDOORI

— ◆ —

Expensive, yes, but for that occasional romantic treat, why not? Here it is as a starter, and to top things off . . . serve it with pink champagne!

Serves: 2 as a starter

7-8 oz (200-225 g) pre-
    prepared raw lobster flesh,
    cut into bite-sized cubes.

7 oz (200 g) red tandoori
    marinade (page 11)

Mix the lobster pieces and the marinade together in a non-metallic bowl. Cover and refrigerate for between 6 and 24 hours.

To cook, preheat the oven to 375°F/190°C/Gas 5. Slide the lobster pieces on to skewers, leaving a slight gap between each piece. Put the skewers on to an oven rack above a foil-lined oven tray and place this in the oven. Alternatively, they can be barbecued. Cook for about 15 minutes, turning at least once. Serve on a bed of salad with lemon wedges, naan bread and tandoori chutney.

TANDOORI TIGER PRAWN

— ◆ —

Huge black striped prawns up to 10 inches (25 cm) long thrive in the Bay of Bengal. Aptly named 'tiger' prawns, they weigh up to 4 oz (110 g) each. Though expensive, they are superbly fleshy and tasty, and a good fishmonger will supply you with them.

Serves: 2 as a starter

2 × 4 oz (110 g) raw Bengal
  tiger prawns, shelled, deveined and washed clean

7 oz (200 g) raan marinade
  (page 13)

Prick the prawns with a fork and coat thoroughly with the marinade in a non-metallic bowl. Cover and put in the fridge for 24 hours maximum.

To cook, preheat the grill to medium heat. Slide each prawn on to a skewer. Put the skewers on a rack above a foil-lined grill tray and place this in the midway position under the heat. Alternatively, they can be barbecued. Cook for about 10-12 minutes, turning at least once. To finish off, raise the tray nearer to the heat and singe the prawns to obtain a little blackening. Serve on a bed of salad with lemon wedges, naan bread and chutney.

TIKKA AND TANDOORI MASALA CURRIES

Any of the recipes on pages 41-43 can easily become a tikka or tandoori masala curry by adding it and any spare marinade to a full portion (16 oz/450 g) of cooked tikka/ tandoori masala curry gravy (page 14). Cook the gravy first, and keep it warm or reheat it.

BROWN SHRIMP TIKKA MASALA

— ◆ —

The traditional British way of buying fresh whole shrimps (or prawns) is to buy them from the fishmonger by the pint. (For the metric minded, this is 600 ml.) Selling by volume allows for considerable variation in density and water content. To be consistent, this recipe weighs tiny brown shrimps which are then cooked with heads off but shells on. Everything is edible. The soft shells give a slight, not unpleasant crunch and the tikka fry adds a highly complementary taste factor.

Serves: 4 as a starter, 2 as part of a main course

1¹/₂ lb (675 g) small raw
  brown shrimps, heads off,
  shells on
3 tablespoons vegetable ghee
  or oil
3 or 4 garlic cloves, sliced
1 inch (2.5 cm) cube fresh
  ginger (optional), finely
  chopped
4 oz (110 g) onion, sliced
3-4 tablespoons red tandoori
  marinade (page 11)
2 or 3 tomatoes, chopped

a few pieces green and/or red
  capsicum pepper, chopped
0-2 fresh chillies (red and/or
  green), chopped
salt to taste
1-2 teaspoons garam masala

SPICES
1 teaspoon white cummin
  seeds
1 teaspoon sesame seeds
¹/₂ teaspoon lovage seeds

Heat the ghee or oil in a large karahi or wok. Fry the **spices** for 20 seconds, then add the garlic and stir-fry for 30 seconds more. Add the optional ginger and continue for 30 seconds more. Add the onion and, lowering the heat, fry for about 5 minutes to allow it to begin to go golden, stirring occasionally. Raise the heat, add the marinade and stir-fry the mixture for a couple of minutes until it changes colour (goes darker), meaning that it is cooked.

Add the shrimps to the pan with the tomatoes, capsicum and chillies and stir-fry for 5-8 minutes until they are cooked. If at any time the dish starts sticking, add a little water to 'release' (but not swamp) it. Salt to taste, sprinkle with the garam masala and serve at once.

TANDOORI PILCHARD

— ◆ —

Other oily fish such as herring or mackerel can be used. Or try snapper for a change. Fresh fish are best for flavour.

Serves: 2

2 fresh pilchards, about 12 oz (345 g) each

7 oz (200 g) green tandoori marinade (page 12)

Gut and wash the pilchards, then dry them. Coat with the marinade and leave for 30-60 minutes.

To cook, preheat the grill to high heat. Put the pilchards on to a rack above a foil-lined grill tray and place this in the midway position under the heat. Alternatively, they can be barbecued. Cook for about 10-12 minutes, turning at least once. To finish off, raise the tray nearer to the heat and singe the pilchards to obtain a little blackening. Serve on a bed of salad with lemon wedges, naan bread and tandoori chutney.

CHAPTER 5

Vegetables

Traditionally only meat or poultry was cooked in the tandoor. Vegetables were never considered worthy. Indeed you will rarely, if ever, find them in the tandoori restaurant. More's the pity because, as the following recipes prove, there are as many delicious tandoori/tikka-style vegetable dishes as there are vegetables. Also in this chapter are recipes using eggs and paneer (see pages 52 and 54-5).

TANDOORI BAKED POTATOES

One of the best vegetable adaptations to tandoori-style is the potato (and its close relatives the yam, sweet potato, swede, parsnip and turnip). It is tandoori marinated, then foil wrapped and slow baked.

Serves: 2 as a snack or to accompany a meal

2 large baking potatoes	*7 oz (200 g) tandoori marinade, red, green or raan (pages 11-13)*

Scrub and peel the potatoes, then poke them deeply with a small thin-bladed knife to assist the marinade to penetrate. Immerse them in the marinade in a non-metallic bowl, cover and refrigerate for up to 24 hours.

To cook, preheat the oven to 325°F/160°C/Gas 3. Ensure that each potato is liberally coated with marinade, then wrap them carefully in foil. Keep the spare marinade for later. Place the potatoes on an oven tray and bake for 1-1¼ hours. Before unwrapping, test that they are cooked by poking a skewer through. If there is no resistance, they are cooked. (If not, carry on cooking.)

Unwrap the potatoes and, keeping them on their foil, pour on the spare marinade and put them under the grill at medium heat to finish them off. Just cook them until they blacken a little bit, turning once. Serve hot, on a bed of salad, with chutney and Indian breads.

SOME VARIATIONS

Try ringing the changes by using other roots and tubers such as small white yam, red sweet potato (American yam), white sweet potato, parsnip, swede, turnip, even uncooked beetroot. Choose a size which you consider is sufficient per person, and follow the previous recipe, adjusting the cooking time to suit the type and size of vegetable (yams, sweet potatoes and parsnips, for example, will take less time than potatoes of the same size).

ROAST TIKKA POTATOES

— ◆ —

The Great British roast potato is a hero among dishes.
Add tandoori marinade and it becomes even more sump-
tuous, especially when served with tandoori roasts. Ghee
improves the flavour.

Choose your potatoes by eye. For roasting they should
be neither too big nor too small. Round ones of about
2-2½ inches (5-6.5 cm) diameter are ideal.

Serves: 4 as an accompaniment

8-12 potatoes (see above)	*ghee or vegetable oil*
7 oz (200 g) tandoori	
marinade, red, green or	
raan (pages 11-13)	

Scrub and peel the potatoes. Halve them and prick them
deeply all over. In a large non-metallic bowl, immerse
them in the marinade. Cover and refrigerate for up to 24
hours.

To cook, place in the hot oven during the roasting of
another roast dish. Judge your timing so that the potatoes
get a minimum of 45 minutes and are ready at the end of
the meat or poultry roasting.

Put the ghee or oil on to an oven tray and warm it in the
hot oven for 5 minutes or so. Shake excess marinade off
the potatoes and keep for later. Place the potatoes on to
the hot oven tray and return to the oven. After 20 minutes
inspect, turn, baste with the ghee and add any remaining
marinade. They should be ready after a further 25 to 30
minutes. Serve with any roast dish.

SOME VARIATIONS

Small white yam, red sweet potato (American yam), white
sweet potato, parsnip, swede and turnip can be roasted
using exactly the same recipe as above. Adjust the cooking times accordingly.

Opposite page 48 (top to bottom): Tandoori Baked Potatoes (**pages 46-7**), Tandoori Chutney – Mint Raita (**page 56**), Asparagus Tikka Stir-Fry (**page 51**), Chestnut Tikka Stir-Fry (**page 51**), and Kulcha Naan (**page 63**)

Opposite (top to bottom): Paneer Tikka on Skewers (**page 55**) served on Peshawari Naan (**pages 61-2**), and Paneer Tikka Masala Curry (**page 54**)

TIKKA DRY
STIR-FRY VEGETABLES

— ◆ —

This technique enables you to stir-fry virtually any vegetable of your choice, to completion in just a few minutes. The use of the tandoori marinade gives the vegetables a distinctive tasty flavour. The choice of vegetables is up to you, but I give suggestions in the five recipes on pages 50-51.

Serves: 4 as an accompaniment

1lb (450 g) prepared vegetables of your choice (see pages 50-1)
2 tablespoons vegetable ghee or oil
2 garlic gloves, sliced
1 inch (2.5 cm) cube fresh ginger, (optional) sliced
4 oz (110 g) onion, sliced
3-4 tablespoons tandoori marinade, red, green or raan (pages 11-13)
2 or 3 tomatoes, chopped
a few pieces green and/or red capsicum pepper, chopped
0-2 fresh chillies (red and/or green), chopped
salt to taste
1-2 teaspoons garam masala

SPICES
1 teaspoon white cummin seeds
1/2 teaspoon black cummin seeds (optional)
1/2 teaspoon wild onion seeds
1/2 teaspoon black mustard seeds

Heat the ghee or oil in a large karahi or wok. Fry the **spices** for 20 seconds, then add the garlic and stir-fry for

30 seconds more. Add the optional ginger and continue for 30 seconds more, then add the onion and, lowering the heat, fry for about 5 minues to allow it to begin to go golden, stirring occasionally. Raise the heat, add the marinade and stir-fry the mixture for a couple of minutes until it changes colour (goes darker) meaning that it is cooked.

While the onion is cooking, blanch the vegetables (or steam or microwave them) just to heat and soften them. Add them to the pan with the tomatoes, peppers and chillies and stir-fry for just a few minutes, until they are as crisp or tender as you want them. If at any time the dish starts sticking, add a little water to 'release' (but not swamp) it. Salt to taste, sprinkle with the garam masala and serve at once.

MANGE TOUT, MOOLI AND SWEETCORN TIKKA STIR-FRY

Serves: 4 as an accompaniment

6 oz (175 g) fresh mange tout, topped and tailed

5 oz (150 g) white radish (mooli), chopped

5 oz (150 g) fresh or frozen sweetcorn kernels

remaining ingredients as in the recipe on page 49.

To cook, follow the previous recipe on page 49 exactly.

CARROT AND PARSNIP TIKKA STIR-FRY

Serves: 4 as an accompaniment

8 oz (225 g) each peeled carrot and parsnip

remaining ingredients as in the recipe on page 49

To cook, follow the recipe on page 49 with the only change being to soften the vegetables for longer.

ASPARAGUS TIKKA STIR-FRY

Serves: 4 as an accompaniment

1 lb (450 g) fresh asparagus, weighed after preparing as described below

remaining ingredients as in the recipe on page 49

Cut off the pithy base parts of the asparagus, if necessary peeling away any further scaly outer parts. To soften, I find the microwave creates the least fuss. Simply place the asparagus in a large enough dish with 1 inch (2.5 cm) of water in it and run the microwave for 3-4 minutes on full heat (650 watt).

Continue with the rest of the recipe on page 49 (omitting the tomato, peppers and chilli if you wish).

MUSHROOM TIKKA STIR-FRY

Serves: 4 as an accompaniment

1 lb (450 g) mushrooms (any type)

remaining ingredients as in the recipe on page 49

No need to blanch or soften the mushrooms, simply clean and peel them if required. Add them after the marinade has changed colour, and follow the rest of the recipe on page 49.

CHESTNUT TIKKA STIR-FRY

Serves: 4 as an accompaniment

1 lb (450 g) cooked and peeled chestnuts (fresh, dried or vacuum packed)

remaining ingredients as in the recipe on page 49

Simply add the chestnuts to the karahi after the marinade has changed colour and follow the rest of the recipe on page 49.

ALOO TIKKA MASALA CURRY

— ◆ —

New potatoes cooked in a rich red creamy sauce which goes well with dry tikka dishes.

Serves: 4 as an accompaniment

*12 oz (350 g) baby new
  potatoes, the smaller the
  better
16 oz (450 g) tikka masala
  curry gravy (page 14)*

*salt to taste
chopped coriander and/or
  mint leaves, to garnish*

Par-boil the potatoes for enough time to get them three-quarters cooked. Make the masala gravy as in the recipe on page 14, adding the par-cooked potatoes at the same time as the tomatoes. Follow the recipe to its end. Salt to taste, garnish and serve.

EGG TIKKA MASALA CURRY

— ◆ —

Hard-boiled eggs make a pleasant change in a curry. Use small (grade 4 or 5) hen's eggs or, for a really interesting dish, use quail eggs.

Serves: 4 as an accompaniment

*8 small eggs (EC grade 4 is 2
  oz/55-60 g)
or 24 quail eggs
16 oz (450 g) tikka masala
  curry gravy (page 14)
salt to taste*

GARNISH
*chopped fresh coriander and/
  or mint leaves
some almond flakes*

Hard-boil the eggs (15 minutes for hen's eggs, 4 minutes for quail's eggs). Make the masala gravy as in the recipe on page 14, adding the shelled and halved eggs to the gravy when you add the cream. Follow the recipe to its end. Salt to taste, garnish and serve.

MIXED VEGETABLES TIKKA MASALA CURRY

— ◆ —

Any vegetables can be used. Here I've chosen frozen mixed vegetables.

Serves: 4 as an accompaniment

16 oz (450 g) frozen mixed vegetables, thawed
16 oz (450 g) tikka masala curry gravy (page 14)
salt

GARNISH
chopped fresh coriander and/ or mint leaves
some shredded fresh or desiccated coconut

To make the masala gravy, follow the recipe on page 14, adding the vegetables with the cream. Follow the recipe to its end. Salt to taste, garnish and serve.

PANEER TIKKA MASALA CURRY

— ◆ —

Paneer is easy to make Indian 'cheese'. It is the Indian version of Chinese tofu (which could be substituted). You'll need rather a lot of milk to make it, but the resultant liquid (the whey) can be used for soups or stock. You'll need up to 2 hours to make the paneer (mostly waiting time) so plan in advance.

Serves: 4

*4 pints (2.25 litres) full
  cream milk (not UHT)*
*4-6 tablespoons vinegar (any
  type) or lemon juice*
*16 oz (450 g) tikka masala
  curry gravy (page 14)*

salt to taste

GARNISH
*chopped or sprigs of fresh
  coriander and/or mint
  leaves*

Make the paneer first. Bring the milk slowly to the boil in a large pan, then add the vinegar or lemon juice, stirring until it curdles. When the curds separate from the whey, strain into a clean tea towel placed on a strainer over a saucepan. Fold the tea towel over and press through the excess liquid. (Keep for later use as stock.)

Now place the curds – from now on called **paneer** – on to the draining board, still in the tea towel. Press it out to a circle about ½-¾ inch (1.25-1.8 cm) thick. Place a flat weight (the original saucepan full of water, for instance) on the tea towel and allow it to compress the paneer. If you want **crumbly paneer**, remove the weight after 30-45 minutes. Crumble the paneer. If you want the paneer to be solid, keep the weight on for 1½-2 hours, then cut the paneer into 16 cubes.

Make the masala gravy following the recipe on page 14 and add the paneer with the cream. Follow the recipe to its end. Salt to taste, garnish and serve.

PANEER TIKKA ON SKEWERS

— ◆ —

This version on the paneer theme uses paneer cubes, marinated, skewered and grilled. To make paneer, follow the method on page 54 to the stage where it is cut into 16 cubes.

16 cubes paneer (page 54)
7 oz (200 g) red tandoori
  marinade (page 11)
8 pieces green capsicum
  pepper, the same size as
  the paneer

8 pieces onion, the same size
  as the paneer
salad
lemon wedges

Follow the previous recipe to make the 16 cubes of paneer. In a non-metallic bowl, combine the marinade with the cubes, then cover and refrigerate for 6 hours.

To cook, preheat the grill to medium. Intersperse eight pieces of paneer on a skewer with the green pepper and onion pieces. Repeat with the second skewer.

Place the skewers on a skewer rack or oven rack above a tray lined with foil. Place this in the midway position under the grill and cook for 3-4 minutes. Turn the skewers and cook for a further 3 minutes. Serve with lemon wedges on a bed of salad.

CHAPTER · 6

—— ◆ ——

Accompaniments

It is usual to serve freshly-made chutneys or raitas such as the Tandoori Chutney below and the Onion Salad opposite, with tandoori and tikka dishes, plus freshly baked naan bread. Rice is also an option. This chapter contains recipes for all these accompaniments, and there's also a recipe for a tasty snack on page 63.

TANDOORI CHUTNEY – MINT RAITA

—— ◆ ——

Any bottled Indian chutneys and pickles also go well with tandoori and tikka dishes, especially the masala curries. The most common are Sweet Mango Chutney, Hot Mango Chutney, Fruit and Nut Chutney, Lime Pickle, Mango Pickle, Brinjal (aubergine) Pickle, Chilli Pickle, Mixed Pickle (a mixture of lime, mango and chilli) and Prawn Balichow Pickle.

Enough for 4

5 oz (150 ml) Greek yoghurt
1 tablespoon chopped fresh
  mint (if available)
1 teaspoon bottled vinegared
  mint

$^1/_2$ teaspoon garam masala
  (page 4)
$^1/_2$ teaspoon turmeric
  (optional)

Simply mix the ingredients together. Chill and serve.

56

TANDOORI CHUTNEY – RED VARIATION

As previous recipe but omit the turmeric and add ½-1 teaspoon red tandoori paste (page 9) to the mixture.

TANDOORI CHUTNEY – GREEN VARIATION

The same as the mint raita recipe (page 56) but add ½-1 teaspoon green masala paste (page 8) to the mixture.

ONION SALAD – CACHUMBER

— ◆ —

A splendid and healthy addition to the tandoori meal. If you want the onion to be translucent (as most restaurants serve it), leave the mixture overnight or longer.

Enough for 4

*1 teaspoon red capsicum
   pepper, finely chopped*
*1 teaspoon green capsicum
   pepper, finely chopped*

½ Spanish onion, thinly sliced
⅓ teaspoon dried mint
*1 teaspoon chopped fresh
   coriander leaves*

Mix and serve.

CACHUMBER RAITA

— ◆ —

A combination of salad and chutney. Simply combine any of the three tandoori chutney (raita) recipes on pages 56-7) with the onion salad recipe above. Chill and serve.

Note: this larger quantity will keep covered in the fridge for 3-4 days.

PLAIN BOILED RICE

— ◆ —

Use Basmati rice, boiled in ample water. Follow this recipe accurately and you'll have fragrant fluffy dry rice.

Serves: 4 (makes 4 portions)

10 oz (300 g) Basmati rice   *3 pints (1.75 litres) water*

Pick through the rice to remove grit and impurities. Boil the water. (It is not necessary to salt it.) While the water is heating up, rinse the rice briskly with fresh cold water until most of the starch is washed out. Run hot tap water through the rice at the final rinse. This minimises the temperature reduction when you put the rice into the boiling water.

When the water is boiling properly, put the rice into the pan. Start timing. Put the lid on the pan until the water comes back to the boil, then remove the lid. It takes 8-10 minutes from the start. Stir frequently.

After about 6 minutes, taste a few grains. As soon as the centre is no longer brittle but still has a good *al dente* bite to it, drain off the water. The rice should seem slightly undercooked. Shake off all the excess water, then place the strainer on to a dry tea towel which will help remove the last of the water.

After a minute place the rice in a warmed serving dish. You can serve it now or, preferably, put it into a very low oven or warming drawer for at least 30 minutes and at most 90 minutes. As it dries, the grains will separate and become fluffy.

Just before serving, fluff up the rice with a fork to aerate it and release the steam.

FRIED PULLAO RICE

— ◆ —

A simple method of making tasty pullao rice by stir-frying plain rice, boiled as in the previous recipe.

Serves: 4 (makes 4 portions)

10 oz (300 g) dry Basmati
  rice, cooked and drained
  as in the previous recipe
1 tablespoon butter ghee or
  vegetable ghee
1-2 teaspoons desiccated
  coconut (optional)
flakes of coconut, to garnish

SPICES
1 teaspoon fennel seeds

¹/₂ teaspoon green cardamom
  seeds
¹/₂ teaspoon black cummin
  seeds
2 star anise
2 inch (5 cm) piece cassia
  bark
2 or 3 bay leaves
2 or 3 cloves

Heat the ghee in a karahi or wok and stir-fry the **spices** for about 30 seconds. Lower the heat and add the rice. Stir-fry until it is hot enough to eat. (If the heat is too high the rice will stick and burn.) Garnish with the coconut and serve at once.

NAAN BREAD

— ◆ —

The traditional bread cooked in the tandoori is called *naan*. It is flat leavened bread, which means it contains an agent, yeast, to make it rise or aerate and therefore become puffy. Cooking naan in the tandoor cannot be bettered. The bread is pressed against the top side wall of the oven and it cooks in a few minutes.

A very hot oven is a satisfactory though somewhat costlier way of cooking naan. The cheaper, equally satisfactory way is using the grill. The latest restaurant trend is to cook the largest possible naan. I heard one such described as a 'naan as large as an elephant's ear'. If you wish to do that, follow the recipe below but don't divide it into four.

Makes: 4 naan breads

2 oz (50 g) fresh yeast, or 3 tablespoons yoghurt	*2 teaspoons granulated sugar*
lukewarm water	*1 teaspoon wild onion seeds (optional)*
1¹/₂ lb (675 g) strong white flour	*melted butter ghee or vegetable oil*

Dissolve the fresh yeast in a little lukewarm water. Put the flour in a warmed bowl, make a well in the centre and pour in the yeast or yoghurt. Gently mix the flour and the sugar and enough lukewarm water to make a firm dough. Remove from the bowl and knead on a floured board until well combined.

Return to the bowl and leave in a warm place for a couple of hours to rise. Your dough, when risen, should have doubled in size. It should be bubbly, stringy and elastic. Add the seeds. Knock back the dough by kneading it down to its original size.

Divide the dough into four equal parts. Roll each part into a tear-drop shape at least ¹/₄ inch (5 mm) thick. Preheat the grill to three-quarters heat, cover the grill pan with foil and set it in the midway position. Put the naan on to the foil and grill it. Watch it cook (it can easily burn). As soon as the first side develops brown patches, remove it from the grill. Turn it over and brush the uncooked side with a little melted ghee. Return it to the grill and cook until it is sizzling. Remove. Repeat with the other three naan. Serve at once.

TANDOORI PASTE NAAN

— ◆ —

A really simple and very tasty variation on the naan bread theme. You can do this to any of the naan bread recipes in this book.

Simply smear red tandoori paste, green masala paste or raan tandoori paste (pages 8 and 9) or one of the marinades on pages 11-13 on the top side of the naan just prior to grilling.

PESHAWARI NAAN

— ◆ —

Peshawar is the town in Pakistan nearest to the Khyber Pass, and it is here that tandoori cooking is said to have originated. What that has to do with this sweet naan, studded with almond flakes and sultanas, I'm sure I don't know, but it is very popular.

Makes 4 peshawari naans

2 oz (50 g) fresh yeast, or 3 tablespoons yoghurt
lukewarm water
1½ lb (675 g) strong white flour
2 teaspoons granulated sugar

1 teaspoon wild onion seeds (optional)
2-3 tablespoons flaked almonds
1-2 tablespoons sultanas
melted butter ghee or vegetable ghee

Follow the recipe on page 60, but once you have rolled out the four naans, sprinkle half the almonds and sultanas over them and press in. Turn over and do the other side. Continue with the recipe to the end.

TANDOORI KEEMA NAAN

— ◆ —

Stuffed naan breads are extremely popular and worth the minimal extra effort to make. This one is stuffed with tandoori spice mince (in the form of the Sheek Kebab mix on page 21).

Makes 4 tandoori keema naan

approximately 6 oz (175 g)   *1 recipe naan bread (page*
    raw Sheek Kebab mix   *60)*
    (page 21)   *7 oz (200 g) red tandoori*
a little vegetable oil or ghee   *paste (page 9)*

Divide the kebab mix into four and flatten each into a thin 4 inch (10 cm) oval disc. Fry the discs in a little oil or ghee in a flat pan until cooked. Allow to cool. Make up the naan dough as in the recipe on page 60 to the point where the dough is divided into four parts. Roll each part out into an oval nearly double the size of the final naan. Smear all over with tandoori paste. Place a kebab disc, off-set to one side, on each piece. Fold each naan over and carefully roll out dough to full size. Continue with the naan bread recipe to cook.

KULCHA NAAN

— ◆ —

Another stuffed naan recipe. Here the stuffing is fried garlic and onion. Time is saved using dried onion flakes.

Makes 4 kulcha naan

1 tablespoon butter ghee or
   vegetable ghee
1/2 teaspoon cummin seeds
4 garlic cloves, sliced

4 tablespoons dried onion
   flakes
1 recipe naan dough (page
   60)

Heat the ghee in a pan. Stir-fry the cummin seeds and garlic for 30 seconds, then add the onion flakes. Remove from the heat at once, stirring until it stops sizzling. Cool before adding to the dough.

Make the dough following the recipe on page 60. Add the garlic/onion mixture to the dough when you knock it back, then proceed with the rest of the recipe.

TANDOORI SCRAMBLED EGG

— ◆ —

Ingenious and simple, it makes an extremely tasty snack at any time. Try it in a sandwich.

Serves: 2 as a snack

4 large eggs
2 teaspoons cream
1 teaspoon butter
1/2 teaspoon cummin seeds,
   roasted

1 teaspoon red tandoori
   paste (page 9)
salt to taste
chilli powder to taste
mustard cress to garnish

Lightly beat the eggs with a fork, adding the cream. Heat the butter in a small saucepan. Pour in the eggs, the cummin and the paste and, with minimal heat, stir until solid but not dry. Sprinkle with salt and chilli powder to taste, garnish and serve hot or cold.